CASCADIA

ALSO BY BRENDA HILLMAN

BOOKS (WESLEYAN UNIVERSITY PRESS)

White Dress
Fortress
Death Tractates
Bright Existence
Loose Sugar

CHAPBOOKS

Coffee 3, a.m. (Penumbra Press)
Autumn Sojourn (Em Press)
The Firecage (a+bend press)

CASCADIA

BRENDA HILLMAN

WESLEYAN UNIVERSITY PRESS
MIDDLETOWN, CONNECTICUT

WESLEYAN POETRY

Published by Wesleyan University Press
©2001 by Brenda Hillman
All rights reserved
Printed in the United States of America
5 4 3 2 1
CiP data appear at the end of the book

CONTENTS

Sediments of Santa Monica 3

El Niño Orgonon 4

(interruption) 6

A Geology 7

Woods' Edge 15

The Y 16

Sweeping the Interpreter's House 17

Hydraulic Mining Survey 18

Shared Custody 19

Styrofoam Cup 21

Dioxin Promenade 22

Adjacent Wounded 23

Dioxin Sunset 24

Franciscan Complex 25

Birth of Lace 26

Haste Makes Channing 27

Sad Cookies 28

Air for Mercury 29

Her Gold Rush 32

Emigrant Gap 33

Never Mindshaft 34

Twelve Vowels 35

The Shirley Poem 36

The White of Action in Literature 44

Past Guinda 45

Pre-Uplift of the Sierra 46

The *(Or: It)* 47

The Formation of Soils 48

Glacial Erratics   49

Fresno Lunette/Predella   50

Frail Substitute   51

The Rise of the Napa Hills   52

Songless Era   53

Curved Knowledge   54

Cascadia   55

Patterns of Paint in Certain Small Missions   61

Breathing in Church   62

Birth of Syntax   63

Noon Chain Replica   64

A Quotidian   65

Left Eye   66

Moths Walking Along   67

Storm Triangles   68

Christ's Height   69

(blank page)   70

Half the Half-Nocturnes   71

Before My Pencil   74

ACKNOWLEDGMENTS/Notes   77

CASCADIA

The poet's destiny is to expose himself to the force of the undetermined and to the pure violence of being from which nothing can be made...but also to contain it by imposing upon it restraint and the perfection of form.

Maurice Blanchot, *The Space of Literature*
(translation by Ann Smock)

L'espace d'or ridé où j'ai passé le temps
(The space of wrinkled gold where I passed the time)

Pierre Reverdy, "Clear Winter"
(translation by John Ashbery)

"But where is the science in all this, Mulder? You're talking alchemy here."

The X-Files

SEDIMENTS OF SANTA MONICA

A left margin watches the sea floor approach

It takes 30 million years
It is the first lover

More saints   for Augustine's mother

A girl in red shorts shakes Kafka's
The Trial free of some sand

A left margin watches the watcher from Dover

After the twentieth century   these cliffs
Looked like ribbons on braids or dreads

A dream had come right over
With a sort of severe leakage

Ah love let us be true to one another

Went down to the ferris wheel
God's Rolodex

There were neon spikes around everyone
Like the Virgin's spikes

Old punk's mohawk   Evidence of inner fire

Rode throwing words off   Red current   Light swearing

Ah love   The century
Had become a little drippy at the end

We're still growing but the stitches hurt   *Let us be*

True to one another for the world

Easy on the myths now
Make it up   Sleep well

EL NIÑO ORGONON

Using cosmic magic and destruction equally
the ocean has decided to rearrange
its syntax so the jet stream
shifts north; its waves warm, its
sentences swell, until life, one of
the yeses between swirls, roundly, in
the form of beach parties with
center-colored balloons full of unused gases
from nearby stars that are suddenly
short of heat, moves to dreamishness,
though movement was actually its second
choice, movement is infinity which failed.

There appeared a small room under
the sea; heat they dumped too
much of lives in there, with
the doomed forms, singing, "Toy sold
separately," he starts these early storms
off San Diego, pushes absorbing action;
they named him boy and make
him metaphorical but he thinks he's
a mistake. Can you move sentences
this way? A horizon is a
type of sentence unmaking syntax denying
its maker in preference for a

sea cave of breathing from, while
on shore, reversible winds drive sanderlings
to make wide use of their
wavelet, the latest theory of narrow
not having been tried. There appeared
a small room under the sea
and in it dwelt impossibility, Rimbaud
and the doomed teachers all, considering
the clash of where we have
dumped heat. Creation doesn't fail though
the meaning sea dies. Kelp-ends disappear
into earliest beginnings. Sentences occluded by

their owners are devoured, a gull
is mistaken for a frisbee, meaning,
years ago. We could have stopped
driving but we didn't. Punctuation like
beach-flies as you walk undyingly past
the perfumed woman and madras-shirted man
who, not knowing dioxin garbage made
the niño's fever worse, hold tight,
palm-treeish seaweed up to admire. Examples
are beautiful anyway. They could have
turned off air-conditioning as they climbed
the hills, we could have been

less comfortable in hotels. Sentences dip
down to the idea as wiggle-rock granite
diving through other granite near Pacifica
borrows infinity layers, driving as we
drove, not meaning to. Distance is
in such an uproar. The boy
wants his ocean to stop melting.
Wants the baby-seal-head-looking surfers peeling off
their wetsuits in the parking lot
at Montara to look up. So
much for the problem of being
unique. Weather was unique, moving to

a sameness; the boy plays insane
music in its head. We welcomed
weather, we wanted each sentence to
have toothy margins more different even
than a snake. Small sizes of
light chime off surfaces to give
great value to stars. Storms unravel
how we wrecked it; color stopped
by, looking blue, purple. Didn't you
feel everything, finally? Weather taught
you to write funny. When it stops
being wrecked, we'll write normally.

(enter: The "we"—)

A GEOLOGY

What we love, can't see.

If Italy looks like a boot to most people, California
        looks like the skin of a person about to sit
        down, a geology.

Consider the Coast Range. We can achieve
        the same results by pushing a pile of wet
        papers from the left and finally
        they were just in love with each other.

Consider the faultline; with only two sides of it,
        how come you never thought of one of them.

A place we love, can't see.   A condition
        so used   to becoming...

(Those who have straddled reference know a map
        will stand for wholeness.)

When you were trying to quit the drug and broke
        in half you said...

And you had to trust it   (that is, needing it)

Landforms enable us to scare. Where
        Berkeley is, once a shallow sea with
        landforms to the west, called Cascadia.
        No kidding. I read this.

A geology breaks in half to grow. A person whose drug like
        a locust jumps across someone's foot, singing—;
        we disagree with D, who hates similes.

The Transverse Ranges holding Los Angeles spit out
            a desert on their hazard side, a power
            transformed from a period of thrall into
            an ordinary period of lying here.

There are six major faults, there are skipped
            verbs, there are more little
            thoughts in California. The piece of coast
            slides on the arrow; down is
            reverse. Subduction means the coast

goes underneath the continent, which is
            rather light. It was my friend. I needed it.
            The break in the rock shows forward; the flash
            hurts. Granite is composed of quartz, hornblende
            and other former fire. When a drug

is trying to quit it has to stretch. Narrow comes
            from the same place as glamor.

A scarp hangs over the edge as it goes from
            Monterey to Santa Barbara. When we
            were trying to quit it had to shout.
            (The rest of our party had gone up ahead.)
            Exaggeration has no effect upon silence.

It took my breath, I gave it willingly, I told
            it to, and the breath listened—

Consider the place of I-80 towards outcroppings.
            When you've gotten to Auburn, a whole
            dog-shaped ground has broken through,

the rock struggling with features, its bachelor joy, caused
            by the power that has kissed you.

What happened, happened a lot. Not to glamorize
             what can't be helped. A bunch of fiery
             islands floated over and sutured themselves to us

a hundred million years ago. I liked

to hold one. Just, really, light it. Put my
             mouth on it.

It's appropriate to discuss features when we speak of California,

daylight's treatment of a sudden

movement in rock. It pretended not to mind. You
             passed him on the path. Miocene lava
             smiled as it ordered the darker

color to sit down.

When he was trying to quit he based his reasoning
             on the way mountains slip. California's
             glaciers never reach the sea. The drug

was trapped in you, and fit. The Klamath mountains love
             the veins of excellent stress, see figure 12.
             Between the time two mountains slip, nothing
             Between two points of resolution, nothing.
             less. A little more
             almost and the slip happened; it happened
             a lot just 30 million years ago.

I saw between the flames four types of instruments:
             with one they touched my mouth,
             with another you touched
             her feet. Rocks of the oldest

time are barely represented. This is the voice
             from the cave, Oleiria. He was coming
             to fuck me but my face had been removed.

The fault went under artichokes in 1982. She talked
           to the permanent fire about it;

what pushes up from under isn't
           named. Or is that "What makes you do this
           to yourself."—What makes you—A language
           caught up under, like a continent.
           She was inhaling though they told her not to.

In the Gabilan Range, small volcanoes erupted
           softly, then this throw-rug-over-the-carpet-
           in-a-bowling-alley type of effect. A california

is composed of moving toward, away, or past; a
           skin is not separate; a poem is

composed of all readings of it. Elements
           redeem themselves plenty, alchemists say so.
           I gave my breath quite easily, then. Sorry it's

ashes, sorry it's smoke all the way down. Gravity
           has to practice. The disciple of angles
           smashed planet after planet, rubbing the cave
           of chalk onto his cue, and put them
           into corners like Aquinas's five
           proofs for the existence of God. Nice
           touch on that boy, nice touch on those
           who sleep till noon, who sleep the sleep
           of the uninsured till noon and wake with maps
           of Sacramento on their hands.

What made the Sierra lift from the right. Telluric Poptart.
           Geologists refer to the range as
           trapdoorlike. It made him cry, he gave it
           willingly, the bartender brought him

free drinks and sent him out into the pale
wrong proud civilian night—

A geology can't fix itself. Nor can description.
Horses run upside down in
the undermath. A power has twinned itself
in that place. We follow it until we are
its favorite, then we live. Does the drug
recover? The Pacific Plate

began this recent movement 20 million years ago. Fresno
was underwater; the small creatures
barely noticed.

She smelled it till it stopped looking pretty; let's call a spoon
a spoon. We dig right down into ourselves
for the rocks of the middle kingdom. Gold

folded into the Motherlode often twinned
with quartz. They seemed to like each other.
Addicts stay on the porch together, lighting them,

and elsewhere, lighthouse cliffs recall the tremors
that brought them there. I *whered*
the wheel and the continent moved over

but I still wanted it.

Los Angeles cheap bedding. You'd allow her
to go first and then you'd go, pull the youngest
blanket over her—bang. If that's
how you like it, fine. Like warm sandstone.

We're living at the dawn of creation as far as
California is concerned. The skin
goes first. Most beaches are losing sand,
it drifts south to Mexico. He sold it, she mixed it, we

bought the *pfft* in 198x, trying to endure
      the glassfront curve in the unaccountable
      ghostman's pleasure. Get down

off that ladder, you. Ceiling stars. Little fiery

islands were light as they ordered Nevada
      to move over. The white thing took
      her breath, she let it slide, it recognized
      what to do. After it started, no
      change; seeing you was methodone
      for seeing you.

The number of faults in middle California
      is staggering—that is, we stagger
      over them till it's
      difficult to follow our own. Each tremor
      is the nephew of a laugh—
      sandstone, shale, chert from the Triassic
      near I-Forgetville. He lined
      them up, they made white sense,

stretchmarks on her body like
      public transportation, very coastal,
      very Sierra traintracks that click-click
      down the sides of thighs, stretchmarks
      where the soul has grown too quickly
      from inside—

But in a way, not really. A geology

has its appetites. New islands are forming
      to get the gist of it. Much of the coast
      moved on its own to get free. Sometimes
      he'd just pass it to you, the prince of stains;
      the universe cried through him. The sea

was glassing itself over Half Moon Bay. Should have
        dropped again suddenly, in the service
        of some burnt out Eden.

It's appropriate to discuss what can't be
        helped. Phyllites, schists, cherts
        marbles. An angel in the annunciation,
        little subzero Mary kneeling
        before you in the bathroom while you were
        burning your skin off.

You went east and you went south. They
        took out their little fear schedules. The Pacific
        Plate on the left moving north while
        the right stands still if you
        look down on it. There's no way

to say progress had been made. I never did

not think about lighting them, not one day,
        as if a requiem could help how chords
        fell out the bottom; Cascadia breathed; I tried
        program, H tried program after program,
        P tried specific harvests
        of bubbles. 12 step ashes. Extra metal

on the stove. The rest of our party
        had gone on ahead. Don't name it. The lithosphere
        likes to float on the aesthenosphere, the soft
        mobile voice of the unseen. *I slide*

below you sweet and high. It wants

to hear you. It wants to touch you. It wants
        to be happy and it wants to die.

Phyllites, schists, cherts, marbles. Press #
      when you are finished. No one knows why
      the arc of minor islands sewed themselves
      to us in that way. When I put it

to my mouth I had no ability to stop it.
      The sea ate the colors a hundred million years ago.

A geology is not a strategy. When an addict tries to leave
      the desire to make himself over shifts from
      what it felt like to have been a subject;

L.A. will dwell beside San Francisco eventually.

Tempting to pun on the word *fault*. All right,
      say *plot*. All right, *happens*. The tendency
      to fault relieves the strain. New islands
      were forming to get the gist of it. We wanted
      the extraordinary stranger in our veins.

Whether it's better not to have been held by something.
      The oldest limestone, prevalent between Big Sur
      and Calaveras, is not "better than," say,
      any other kind. The suffering wasn't luckier,
      it wasn't a question of asking.

In the instead hour, the minutes of not recovering
      from the difference of what we loved;
      sameness is also true: stone like a spider

sucking the carapace the same color as itself.

In the expiation of nature, we are required to
      experience the dramatic narrative of matter.

The rocks under California are reigning in their little world.

This was set down in strata so you could know
      what it felt like to have been earth.

WOODS' EDGE

Infinity lifted:
a gasp of emeralds.

I thought I felt
the tall night trees
between them,

no exactitude,
a wait not even
known yet.

I held my violet up;
no smell.
It made a signal squeak
inside, bats,

lisps of pride;

ah, their little things,
their breath: lungs of a painting,

they swept me
in four ways, their square
plans, as I have made
a good square saying,

you I
you not-I
not-you I
not-you not-I,

ritual of hope
whose weight
has not been measured—

THE Y

They are bringing back the bones of Che Guevara
      so the system of universal capitalism
      will be reversed while a girl on the stairmaster
      reads *Anna Karenina*, pausing at the part
      where Vronsky, thinking Anna into the wrong coldness,
      might turn his back on her another time. The girl
      would name her dog for him if she had one. Legs with
      many tattoos of heavenly bodies (ceiling
      stars, moons, snakes) push weights; it all shakes, and east of here,
      aspen forests growing from root systems that never
      die send out shoots above ground anyway because
      the lust to be individual exceeds the
      desire to lie down anonymously above
      a mantle of fire. No one's arguing about
      formal necessity or the power below
      survival or if they wanted to be touched, there.

SWEEPING THE INTERPRETER'S HOUSE

An individual

transgressive arrow

is shot

through everything;

the six-gendered wind

wipes it away.

Nightshade, infinity:

against you

to get to you—

Now   a fly

smoothing its gloves

for the black prom

HYDRAULIC MINING SURVEY

Whether or not radiance has intention,
yellow was brought from the caverns
in a series of baseline laughs.
A system of coax-coax, granite glowed
and drove gold up between its
legs of quartz. Gray was only

part of it. A wedge of black against each swirl like congressional signatures as you stand between stope blocks. Gold just didn't want to. If you touch the already rusted without permission type pump near Emigrant Gap you're pointing down with it. It killed peasants, with them. Drained whole streambeds, washed half mountains down to pay for the Civil War till 1878 the Delta was impassable from this. The spirits coughed at xenolithic odds. They had meant to do it in their rooms. Whole cliffsides moved in salmon paths when they met their sister, poor river. Poor forever having to act like this. In a hundred

years, people were using Visa to
pay off MasterCard. And still
the earth's thinking in flecks. River
meetings take place anyway. It's hard
to address water. If you meet
the unpunished dead, avoid cliché.

SHARED CUSTODY

An example often used to show ?? is x falling feet first into a singularity with a
watch on. Fate is what happens backwards. With regard to Persephone,
the seasons don't change till something agrees to her sacrifice.

When a child is dropped off in front of the other parent's house she creates a
history of space and yellow hurrying in the unopposed direction as we
learn to read by hurrying meaning.

She got out of the car. Smell-threads of Johnson's baby shampoo. Redolence exists
by itself as opportunity. The end of the Cold War had come. In Russia,
more oranges, lizard baskets of capitalism. I tried to talk to her father; he
tried to talk to me.

As x falls by prearrangement with the experimenters, yellow is unopposed. The
child, leaving the car, drops an alphabet on the path. y. e. l. Shaving of
yellow, central plaid, black from a fraction if she has been brave about
including the math.

She hated her little bag. A Thursday humming followed. My writing was falling
apart. She was learning to read.

A fate begins to be assembled when the linear is shared. All it does doesn't work.
Should dirt not praise her efforts? Little pointed

arrows swerve around the (from the mother's perspective) vanishing skirt. Flashes
of letters here. Here. Home is the fear of size. A word can fall apart. y. e.
We sat in the car. Tiny bats between Berkeley double-you'd the air.

The lip of a singularity is an event too far beyond, good corduroy with its highs
and lows as the star dissolves in the just-having-spun and you're not
supposed to ask how x feels as he falls in. Persephone practices her yes,
her no, her this that and the other, the child approaching the house of the
father in motion of minutes, free for twenty yards of both of them, makes
a roof with her good-bye: // bye \\ mom. They'll have to invent new
seasons to explain it.

A daughter grows a horizon. Somehow a line by which a life could be pursued.

When she started to read, I no longer heard language, it heard me. I had the stupid
idea that she should dress up to leave.

x should have checked with Persephone about the kicking and screaming. I should have checked with the mother but I was the mother. Backward should try to fix loss so it is not devastation but chronicle.

Panic plaid, almost at his door, *I cannot see what flowers are.* Daffodils. Dirt's birthday candles. California is medium old. *x* won't be very young when he gets to the center, nor will the child, testifying to cloth, dropped, sent back fractal, active as the buoys on the bay, nor is the child very young.

If you are time you think in terms of next. If you are Persephone you think in terms of dirt. If you're the metaphor you'll let the thing stand for it. On Monday the flash of a dove, your hoping

frame. The child *can* look back, the myths don't apply here, if you think one joy was sacrificed it's because you said it. What choice did it have when the thing undid but to call her in broken colors.

STYROFOAM CUP

thou still unravished   thou

thou,   thou bride

thou unstill,

thou unravished   unbride

unthou   unbride

DIOXIN PROMENADE

Colors get married and dancesteps try
but a dancestep is selfish. Diagrams
make dioxin look like a six-sided
dance with carbon prongs but dancesteps
won't build up over time. Some of
the white leaks out, a strangeness

we can't recognize till marshes resemble
more rheumy stanzas but unchosen. Dioxin
likes breastmilk. Daylight braids in equal
roses on both sides around people
fishing near Unocal in the battered
colors of secret julys, colors dreamed

in the dreamathon before we sprayed
those brownskinned people with our pink
so why was it called agent
orange in sixty-eight? State poppies try
to convert it to themselves but
there's some cross-over. An interviewer asks

where a poem starts. He's disturbed
about the stanza. Its beauty
subverts intention. Little worlds are
images of big ones, crimes have
poets, a metaphor is meant to
self-destruct. Dioxin stays in a body

seven years, a lump forms in
the friendly tissue near her heart
like the last time she wants
to see someone's car. Lovers of
seafood, dockworkers, a swan named Myrtle
wade in Richmond's moat, the queen

is sick, her lord the chamberlain
is taking note, tearing up sentences
to make them clean. When you
danced, did you count or just
want to get out and drive
south, to be continually seen, seen?

ADJACENT WOUNDED

The eye forgets the eye

A crow scoops up more red as it flies by

Sight stops other categories

Other fathers had the wrong Mary

People working in the right-hand fields

Tule sheathing   for rooves   let wind care

Lamb   Lamb

Rubbing the little future

Voice ink
Voice-nik

Hunted in the house of air

San Juan Bautista
1797

DIOXIN SUNSET

There was a hurt that lay between two colors,
   a shade not resolved in the mind
   because it is the mind.

An envy had tried to exceed itself
   in the marsh between pink and orange.

You don't let it, you blend them; in this, the contract
   to live anyway.

               (sequence of)

Past farms—*(sequins of)*—past rows
   as satisfying as running a thumbnail
   on the tines of a dimestore comb.

Wispy haze near Paso Can't-tell-yet,
   a mission where the earth's throat was sore.

Pink can be proud when you see it, making conquests,
   the double ") (" of
   a confident sun Drake must have watched going down *(seasons of)*
   first as a vase, then as a pan.

Once you commit to a color, you take on its weakness: life:death, 2:1.
   Its power was so great we could not kill
   our envy. (Why won't other
   painters say this.) In talking back to the runny
   coast, new actions form.

               (glow)

FRANCISCAN COMPLEX

Each day the job gets up
And rubs its eyes

We are going to live on in dry amazement

Workers push the granite bed under the avenue

Bed of the married
The re-   the pre-married

Making a form as forms become infinite

The scrapings   scraping

Graywhacke   chert

People wait for their bumpy little pizzas
Theories of theories in gravity voices

Melpomene goddess of tragedy bathes

Mostly the bride never the bridesmaid

Angel food in whole foods

Consider Tanguy whose lunar responses to childhood
Made everything a horizon

Those walking upside down don't know what to think

The finch engineering itself to deep spring

Or you   life   tired of being cured

How many layers
Of giving up are there

One of it

Two of everything in the arc you save

BIRTH OF LACE

When we'd finished counting the begats we'd begin
to draw the cosmos in the church bulletin;

Something was wearing a brenda's brain out &&&&&
making curls on the outside.

The little mama looked on
with a western idea of progress,

trying as an individual, in a fervent series;

our next went usefully awry to dream, as needed.

A small mark gets through unscathed. Lace
is a female genre; parsing sentences with Lyn and Nat, drip down now,

catkin selves with slanty, slanty participles

like hazel Yeats thought magic. A self: not to know or to keep one.

It prayed by looking till design talked.

San Luis Obispo
1772

HASTE MAKES CHANNING

On Wednesdays the Coast Range tilts toward the left. Berkeley cracks
   a little more near Dream Fluff after the dentist;

            ("but the work's demand is circular")—

His cellphone was ringing into the mocha;

a general brightness—;   (of xylocaine,   or

                  in Donne's "The Relic,"
                     the bright hair—)

Several trends inside the main idea.   Then

Cody's fans spinning over revolutionary bodies that don't
   believe in the *I* any longer.

The magican saw the little town in the *splendor solis*, tight blue bushes
   wound round like wishes.

SAD COOKIES

The Staff brings in the scrolly silver urn
Jefferson written all over it

Cookies arranged in a circle like the Irish Peace Accord
The kind with the weird red jam in the center

The First Lady talks about the arts

There is no president of cookies

They have the kind of steady thinking
That could accommodate theory

Pssst   eagle   Come down off that wall
There are choirs behind the next day

Blanchot: *The poet's destiny is to expose himself*
To the force of the undetermined

Airline magazine from 1967:
Exaggerate your uniqueness
Expose yourself to things you might avoid

Can't walk in a circle because the corridors of power
Can't not look because of JFK

A third of the invisible can go through closed doors if you let it

The First Lady talks about the national cabin

Think of the *Enquirer* headline:
SWITCHED GIRLS WILL STAY PUT FAMILIES AGREE

Double Jeopardy category   Sweet Nothings for $200
Sweet nothing surrounded by anything

What is a poet's destiny?

AIR FOR MERCURY

I.
After the double party
for the poorly loved

when the gleam in the hound's eye
fell like glass rain on the south

lawn of the countergarden, when
the image of false flags sank

in the mirrored plaques,
when the mirrored plaques

had been passed in, they took
your days and gave them back,

before you unsnapped first
the crenellated shoulder wings

then the fumbling then the little
ankle wings and sent them back

to the wing patrol, in the box,

in the metal box, in the genital
mouth of the rose (the open forms

of the state left so
undone that you were stranded

on the nonimperial coast having
a boat unnamed for you)

you were free, you were
having a bout of meaning—

II.
A leaf hurried by on its
side. Of what is knowledge made?

A season stopped by without your
noticing, saying, lost file, breath boy;

the sun had leaked its power
into things, and all notation had

become inaccurate suddenly, you'd been trying
to talk to them from this

coast, you'd been trying to help
them in their small groups.

III.
Monsters of will and monsters of
willlessness confront the garden; a dragon

crow greets the dusk with its
prow. Rhyming is a tool of

friendly desperation. The spirits will return
though they're not here now.

IV.
Oracles, iron, the misuse of fire
under the young earth, and this

business of being infinitely swept up
in possibility so when you put

your hand down on something white
you noticed that detail, punctuated by

luckless forms. But night had been
deployed: see-through parts of the moon:

lace, *anima mundi*; and weren't there
two forevers, words and space, between

which more *experience* might ride, unencumbered?
You were supposed to tell them

what they'd missed; they'd read your
logics, your letters. So little space

between your letters, the words couldn't
easily air themselves. Remember going back

and forth between the rooms? Blue,
green; the wings had been adjusted.

You were meant to take black
netting off a face or two. Take

something. Passion brought you
here; passion will save you.

HER GOLD RUSH

undry   assigned

    a center

whether   to have been

   given notice for

      the movement in

to which they

      ascribed now   (in their fury)

(in the mines)   modified

   bleached meaning   to debride

    fame   scraping

     metal off

         reconverted to

    the vertical

     the workers

    sending boxes up

      (that very

  oddness dowry)

pulled by your

   fiancé   reality

EMIGRANT GAP

undry

terrified by
the arrangement of
literature

l'epicenter
two kinds of gone

       the opposite

a   of trying
       takes over

e

       hope

oo   comes   a glancement
       tamer

u

NEVER MINDSHAFT

undry   fueled by

     the little efforts

    delayed prank

    separable earth

reality divided

   sworn cascade   where

   you are it

        once was

till   was   unmade

    scattered   (hope's

skidmark   tight

   ecstasy)   chthonic   gold

it   folded   gone

    under now

TWELVE VOWELS

undry   her
gold rush
ruled by
dirt talking

             its urge
             abyss foreman
a   has a key   a
o
i   u
e   where it is you   e
             once were
uu   now called
uuu   into insatiability

THE SHIRLEY POEM

I.
Physical earth reveals itself as persons.

That's what a body is, an
    opportunity, hills dismantled geologically, shifting into
    twiceness now, its wishes hearing—

a landscape full of an original
chaos but not in itself divine.

We'd lived by the words of
    others so when we read accounts
    of the gold rush we weren't
    even sure anymore who was rushing.

"So original" had been a tempting
    idea to go into (images of
    striking solitary gold); trouble is, you
    have to keep doing it. Preferable
    to join the mantle of mud
    and sound, where names let go;

and it's still as much of a
    dream as you can manage, a
    measure meaning nothing and the world.

II.
Hot water pushed quartz and gold
    in solution through magma to surface
    as sunbeams and as wedding rings.

Reconceiving bodies, we call them "veins."
(We write in 'a similar vein.')

Shirley, a doctor's wife traveling to
    California in 1851, writes of her
    "geological deficiencies" and delights in "everchanging
    surfaces" when she's just arrived at
    the new camp called Rich Bar.

Men are filling pans with dirt;
    "I gather from their remarks that
    these bars are formed by deposits
    of earth crowding the river aside
    occupying a portion of its bed."

A solution to an individual is reading more.

Of course there was no mother
    lode; of course it was unlikely.

III.
Recovering from an individual as one reads,
     eyes too busy to go backward.

Shirley, who hasn't made it far
     into history, writes to her sister
     in a lively, modest style imitating
     Bret Harte's literariness, of the death
     of Mrs. B., a miner's wife.

Reading at night (if you're tired):
     like a pickaxe, the eye falls
     on each word. It makes holes
     in a territory. (Some were amazed
     when some others at the conference
     claimed their stylistic territory.) From inside
     the claim, a mineral-self leaks out.

—The text of a woman's body
—The body supported by two buttertubs
—The woman's coffin of unstained pine
—Unstained pine lined with white cambric

Little Mrs B., unimpressed by exterior
     dramas and wreaths of thoughtful snowflakes.

A dead woman, as when we
     lie down to read at night,
     to read among those who've lived.

IV.
It was a common habit for
    miners to bury their money (Re-bury?)

We fall in love with what
    we deem to be good (*deem*
    is a kind of Shirley word).
    The world thinks earth is good,
    and gold is the best earth
    (still trying to understand money).

Shirley watched them panning through gravel
    in valleys of seasonal influence on
    the East Branch of the North
    Fork of the Feather River, contenting
    herself with a philosophy of fortitude,
    waiting, making bookcases from candle crates,
    reading Coleridge, "who is never old."

Witnessing the hanging of a thief
    —"wound around his green-leafed gallows"
    —"a harmless, quiet, inoffensive person"
    (hoping he's not guilty so he'll
    feel less bad at being hanged).

Outside the Oroville motel, a transubstantial
    turning: grackles like computers starting up
    in earth, the crystals stuffed with
    water which makes moltenness unlikely.

(p. 116) "It is almost like death
    to mount to my favorite spot."

V.
The change in a woman's body
    is the change in a california.
    Gold seeps at its own pace
    as though the body were dead.

In the twelfth letter where she
    calls potatoes and onions *vegetables*: "Have
    we not got quintals of dreadful
    mackerel fearfully crystalized in black salt?"

(Shirley having averted American values.)

(She has been valued for her
    description of blue brandy bottles being
    used to replace windows. For us:
    the window *reading*, the window *writing*.)

Shirley's exactly in love with the
    insouciant fiddle player who moves away.
    These butterflies have orange guitar picks
    on their wings and play this sentence:

minds are more heat. The imagined
    reader that exists in the mines
    or holes of the future is
    enchanted as other women will read
    it surely after our next death.

VI.
You can read at the counter
　　of Oroville's (they pronounce it) Corn-you-copia
　　Restaurant while Cindi carries a plate
　　of positively metamorphic-looking biscuits and gravy.

The future had poked some holes
　　in the mine with its fork.

Temporary crush on the East Branch
　　of the North Fork of the
　　Feather River but shouldn't it be
　　tines of a fork? Temporary crush
　　on the fry-cook because of his
　　Denver omelette. Permanent crush on the dead.

Shirley: "Now know, proud Rio de
　　Las Plumas, that these men whose
　　futile efforts you had gloriously defeated…"
Shirley: "…poker, euchre, whist, and ninepins…"

Taking the book outside. Learning to
　　read in the car, keeping it
　　flat. Stoned on interior distances and
　　moderate ravings of E's "alcoholic boy
　　music"—we develop new methods of

searching in the West, having stopped
　　being tormented by nature's body because
　　of not being able to tell
　　which of the living we are.

VII.
Nobody works a claim alone. In
      1851 law arrives; government hasn't yet
      been invented. Forty feet around a
      claim. This need to be unique
      has mostly made us miserable.

In mining operations, dirt is moved
      constantly by spadesmen through a series
      of descending troughs and sieves of
      a three-tiered apparatus only to end
      in what's called a "riddle." Hard
      not to think self-pity is descent.

Usually we hear the dead perform
      but they have to remain half-here,
      active in dirt's community.

A replica of a mining machine
      has been made into a planter.

Brilliant girly Shirley nearly forgotten now—

The woman at the campground market
      knows about Shirley's description of the
      muletrain coming down the canyon with
      supplies. The gay ringing of bells
      reminds her of salty longed-for weddings.
      I married all women in books.

VIII.
Shirley's quite the celebrity to old
    men sitting at in lawn-chairs near
    the hand-painted PAN FOR GOLD sign.

The Feather River bottom has scads
    of fool's gold you can grab
    if you try to touch it
    like experience. It vanishes. Like experience
    it doesn't leave. "I never did
    care much for water in the
    abstract," she writes near the end,
    "though it's useful to make coffee."

The other originality used every speck.
    Nature has your same mind. When

the light is retracted they come
    back. Radiance is definitely a drag
    if voices can't be braided around
    the edge of a dirty paradise.

"I have a vague idea that I
    hooked that butterfly comparison from somebody.
    If so, I beg the injured
    person's pardon, and he or she
    may have a hundred of *mine*
    to pay for it." (*italics hers*)

The springtime asphalt was already hot.
    Some wings got slightly stuck to it
    when they tried to take off.

THE WHITE OF ACTION IN LITERATURE

The bank's awning
Puts stripes in the zeroes

Cafe breath between wordlings
White as eggshells left by raccoons

Rhombus of moonlight siphoned from a lily

Always confusing bridge and bride

;;;?( ),—!.

How can you sleep with that train turned up all night

Main thing is un-unwanting to live
Canaan's pendentive breath so inviting

Hard not to cross when one side
Wanted to be the bridge

PAST GUINDA

The temporary, remade milder,
into permanence—

(that's just fine
   for wood nymphs
    sitting on their stumps).

An ice age shredded tweedy serpentines.

In walnut groves, black coils approaching ground.

Those girls needed your taboos,
oo's cast from *good* to *noon*.

You, life,

poured life and medium life into splotchy cups;
drank one of them.

PRE-UPLIFT OF THE SIERRA

Hermit thrush ,??;;&~   (having chosen the wrong female)—

(Queen Lear,
sometimes sometimes
sometimes sometimes sometimes)—;

had stopped
having respect for time, not for color or substance.

Cher taking it back about being sorry she's fifty.

Eight blues at Meeks Bay not counting the four skies;

others tried to *be* so they stuck to one thing;   sorry, not today.

The faultline is god's palm being read under the sand
where the families are lying:

heartline~   head—

an obsession helpless in the face of ecstasy.

It was August   glacial debris   pieces

of a life reminiscing about the pre-uplift:

outcrops of mudstones and shales,

harmony;

a woman washed her black hat in the lake:

"Anytime you mainstream a hat to the family
there's always a risk."

What is the half-life of having one?

I was half-listening to infinity
when we spoke.

Every sentence was the skin of heaven.

THE *(OR: IT)*

A translator   trying   not to decide   God's gender:

       "wretched was"
    his/her   (or: it)—vaguely,

like ordering from a truckstop menu. A strip of

    panting—or dripping—behind the putative world.

The other gender breathing   without permission.

THE FORMATION OF SOILS

For forty million years   a warm, warm rain—

then the sea got up to try to relax.

Vulnerable volcanoes had just melted away.

He worked below, translating the author's imps and downs,
      his ups and demons—;
pines grew skyward though the pines were not.

Thus began long episodes of quiet,

nickel laterites not ready
for the slots.

It took periods of soft showers attacking the dream
under the silt-covered sun,

Osiris washing his fragments,
Leda swimming with her vagabonds.

Everyone is made essentially the same way.

Through notebooks of tight red dirt
Franciscans walked upside down under us:

aluminum oxides,   incidents of magma,

and I had to go down in the earth for something—

Iron sediments spread over the foothills where Caliban
had his flat;

I was wearing the brown sweater when we spoke,
my heart and the one below translating his heart out.

But by that time, what.

Experience had been sent up, at an angle.

GLACIAL ERRATICS

The last ice age had been caused by a wobble.
After it passed they made houses from stars;

Visitors would peer in
And see the tongs not slipping,

Roomsized pebbles having been moved far.

It's like this more
When we speak than when we write;

Loving thus we have been
Loved by ground,

The word being
A box with four of its corners hidden;

Everything else is round.

FRESNO LUNETTE/PREDELLA

Brown moon rubbed on a tallow mare

Day catching something it liked to be

Shredded music Safer in the car
A piece of the left margin slipped under the sea

Dirt = guts of a star

An ago ago in a new idiom
I was cut off by a car named Stanza
Cut off by a van named Odyssey

The Great Basin sank
The anti-rose rose Filled it with salt

Lettuces fought

Agamemnon   Agribusiness

Unions
A little betterment

St. Agnes held by hair
St. Agnes covered with flame

Loving God
Is like burning burnt matches
Syllables pass A tautology

What if earth had stopped earlier
Not very territory is best

Tractor running over its shadow foot

Tannish orchard
The busy sound of actually

(Right before
seat belts: do you recall being
merged with the driver?)

* * * * * *

FRAIL SUBSTITUTE

Outside the camphor and the unguentine
(We walked under the lintels)

Inside the ledgers of secrecy
(The archer's assistant)

Yes by marking on white
The mindless happiness

Yes then a crater of yeses
A mindless mindless depression

Those who assemble the ropes
Then-ing   Now-ing

Yes to notify the bee
Beside the central Fresno orchard

Yes to unmortify the rose
(Tired of the work the day)

And when she was beheld
(The alloy the willless

The violent vegetal bloom
Under the great fan

Her starch black dress her
New blue flute)

The night can't but a day
Might a day might

A day always
Sends a substitute

* * * * * *

Nuestra Señora de la Soledad
1791

THE RISE OF THE NAPA HILLS

The sea has receded a little. Mild layers stack up
without panic, like e-mail. Twin frenzied suns watch the ocean
sediments settle under Oakville Grocery. Flittery
strings tied to the tops of young vines shimmer two versions of
the actual: red, white. The curfew vintner walks below,
tapping smooth metal vats with a spoon. He asks them the twelve
questions: *Did you love your life? How 'bout now? Can you recite
the table of sunsets? Did the weather wait for you? Did
you wait back? When he shook before the world did you shake too?
Did you fall in the milky sunshine? Do you hear their
gritty theories still? Would you like a drink? Can you live in
two directions with the border guards? You're not answering.
Why didn't you fight more? Didn't you love being bad?*

SONGLESS ERA

A fine ash obscured the sun.

Leaves grew large as rooms.

Stamped recreants strolled near the pond of wands.

There was a great and terrible brightness
    that was pretty much like a fire
    but it had *lots of eyes* in it.

Four syntaxes correspond to four styles of going on.

Can you hear? (How 'bout now.) Non-chanson:

lie down in the tent of a servant-queen;
lie down in the dust; go on.

One kind of sentence remembers the accident;

one kind of sentence is a scar.

CURVED KNOWLEDGE

Those children lost in caves when you were a child—
the town stopped looking for them too soon, as now
we have to accept whatever negotiators decide. If the universe
is curved out like a saddle, the spaceship won't return
and if it's curved in it will. At least a
tolerable thing, we thought, to stop a sob where slackness
crawls. (Some were taken back repeatedly, some not so much.)
They had fallen among lavender, pimply columns, tonsured stalagmites or
a queen's mythy limestones to shine their lights up and
across, though whether the subject gets rescued or not
it confines itself to caverns, not knowing how to end,
aware of the thrill of not knowing. They could have
thrown a rock in first to the mezzanine, a floor
devoted to change panthers, shadows, and middle ferns the ice
maiden walks by with small warm toes but why would
they have tested it? What doesn't live there? Don't you?
A friend says white should be confined to certain rooms
in certain houses, of which the heart is four. Hopkins,
in love with the scalloped sense of a hawk. Bandits
stored gold where children, not going after it,
fell, and if the town stopped looking for you too
soon, there you were, stuffed in the promise of Night
don't joke like that anymore, hold the blue mirror
up, you get to keep the thing you love—

CASCADIA

Prior to 130 million years ago much of California lay beneath ocean waters. It was bordered on the east by the mainland of North America and on the west by a land mass known as Cascadia.

Robert Durrenberger, *Elements of California Geography*

In the search for the search
During the experiments with wheels
Holiday Inn After the scripted caverns
When what had been attached
Lompoc Was no longer attached
After choosing the type of building
hydrangea In which no one has died
We recalled a land or condition
one of those Whose shape was formal
teeth bedspreads Formality gave pleasure
A shadow's shadow dragged it
Back to the sea of eyes
most natives A poem floats inside its margins
They are death and birth receding
say Lom-poke Beauty is not an impasse
Better not to blame
The loved one for a slip
made glad God had a slip of not existing
All girls are an island
Capri Motel Those trucks on 101 with reclining
Ojai Decals of flame and smoke
The willless breath outshocked her
In Chualar a boy threw up
an under- Behind a case of Coke
In the search for the east to admire
nevered spider & After reconsidering which was west
In an era of not singing
At the school of lyric abstraction
pre-Naugahyde The skin of an unthought is thought
After kissing Los Angeles once
chair The landmass known as Cascadia
His parents pick strawberries for us
The *I* caused flagrant slipping
marbleized *Sing sank sunk* in the Something-ocene
sidetable Earth started out loose
Pretty loose   just debris

a shape-shaped   California motels sometimes have
Colonial type scallops in the moulding
inner courtyard   The boy must have been hot
The business of margins waiting
Country Inn   What must Drake have thought
and Suites   When he strolled past the bankruptcy office
Marigolds on the boardwalk
Costa Mesa   The back of a poem is brighter
Than the back of a painting
Osiris rode a ferris wheel
Ophelia rollerbladed
couch having   Syntax is the understudy for infinity
They don't know what caused Cascadia
its horizon   As the arrangements became larger
The lyric had become depressed
remote   Abalone chips in the sidewalk
control   There were little mirrors in his spine
As he threw up
teabag   Do you still love the sentence
Aristotle's four causes of change
Formal Material Efficient Final
And what of the warbler latitudes
And what of the unknown where
The inexhaustible plays against form
Four Points   A compass went south of crazy
Missions indicated by green squares
The skin of a thought is a thought
Saint   Torn earth is better than conquerors
Monica   His parents pick strawberries for us
He picks strawberries for us
On where Cascadia slid
to sing   and   We found a glassy spot to be assembled
A merging subverts the categories
to conceal   Some words shouldn't marry
Consider *flow* for example
And the unmarried rocks

In the east for the search to admire
We spoke the stuttering the slurred
Spiky poplars near Atascadero

Motel 6   Rose to protect the empty
Some moths live only two hours
Formal cause means definition

Lost Hills   Means ask your friend in the blue shirt
Why Cascadia's hair is noisy
In issues of representation

dandelion seed   He threw up from being sick
cream   When the land mass had slid under
After a feathered response

shower   Water running in the motel
To get the being stained out

Fame   The immortal precedes the left margin
A million pagers not working

corrugated wind   A satellite had turned left
Into a round-sided life

Best Western   A truck turned left at the Pacific
   Village   Inn   A sofa-unit in its flat-bed
A line is a unit of attention

Fresno   California's lines so separate
The dirt was heard chip-chipping

our girl such a   Silicon A forbidden wren
The second cause of change said the search

Neo-Platonist   Material cause what it's made of
The Countess of Tripoli listened

song not   Don't try to get the stain out
The red made you live faster

a   No longer eating strawberries
He had another call coming in

thought   Nestled down in the paisley pattern
The island proposed a merger

Then did   Half-moon Dewy and the Secret Julys
Cascadia didn't merge it floated
His song survived his supply

	She peeled back the skin of meaning
	Change has four causes slid Aristotle
La Quinta Inn	The boy hardly bent throwing up
Redding	He had little mirrors in his spine
	Material cause means why
nun-colored	Because of what
	All boys are an island
channel-changer	In issues of representation
	Had a pretty good head on her shoulders
magpie	His head made up of singing
	Loss of meaning is made up
nunning by	Of two things loss and meaning
	Phenomenal accuracy as a moral stance
	Kildeer love the really shitty fields
	Near the missile-testing site in Lompoc
	They run past drought tolerant gardens
	The talk of the town
Radisson	Shirley flies a plane in that one
	Nail City Bravo Pizza Taco Loco
San Diego	The beyond sang the anti-lyric
	His parents pick strawberries for us
	He picks strawberries For us
To will	World champion Nafta unacceptable stain
	The cloud of unknowing knew
the future panicked	In the search for the C in Cascadia
	She felt chastened by angularity
	Credit unions offering farm credit
anti-song	Damselflies over ferrous chloride
	The land mass coddled the sea trench
	They turned right into the argument
	Switching to de-caf was the problem
	Cercamon and Peire Cardenal
post-Naugahyde	Material cause what it's made of
truth	Fat-free chocolate envelope
	I'll be good mama you can come out
	In heaven we'll be recognized

The left had a fear of margins
Some moths live only two hours

Country Inn
And Suites
From flying low in the fields
The face-shaped vault of infinity
Her address was mad at her

Powerbar
It wasn't just the not singing
We anguished it up and released it

I laughed or
Whatever gets old and scary
Baja snapped off at Malibu

it cried
Which rhymes with pale blue
Tattoos on the backs of nymphettes
We could have been happy sooner

Californians aren't good at merging

Ellis Motel
Little mirrors in his spine
Cascadia didn't merge it floated

Tulelake
Why did the chicken cross the ocean
Get someone to help you do it
A poem touches its margins gently
Twelve=the waltz X 4 causes

Formica
kitchenette
The scrub jay cracks seeds for hazel
Thought it was Charlie knocking
We'll eat no more strawberries
She thought envelopes are fattening

after the owl
Her letters arrived unsealed

In the trench for the east to admire
In one motel was a gooey spirit

true
Read *The Highwayman* as children
Black-haired woman tied up

Naugahyde
Shoots herself to warn him
They'll write in the noir of heaven
The Ojai mountains near Jane's house
Quiet as the soul of Because
Too much earth for each strawberry
The little seeds get stuck in your teeth
On earth they will be noticed
And all the human themes

In recognized it will be heaven
The final cause of change said Aristotle
The reason to which things tend

Quality Inn
The beyond is made of the beyond
She had a face lift on her hands
Space prone punctuation driven
The change didn't sink it floated
You of missing cities
The island sang right in slow motion

bath gel
They'd call this their great lost love
But the cliff knows
Where to find the ocean

Executive Inn
People think poets make poems
Poems make poems lying down

shower cap
The final cause the Goddish reason
There's a song that sang all night
There were mirrors in his spine
He bowed like California
Todos los dios estan una isla
This accidental May
Didn't fear the right margin

Country Inn
The reason to which things hover
In the next millennium
Don't wake your sleeping brother
In the earth for the search

And Suites
After considering which was west
They came upon a piece of land

shoe cloth under
It had fragments in its spine
It had everything you wanted

soap
In the tablets on which it was written
There's a space that sings all night

little soap
Not knowing the lyric was broken
The sun looking pretty strange
Lying down on 101 it floated

little
You want to or you don't
soap
Want to change but you'll change

60

; ; ; ; ; ; ; ; ; ; ;   ; ; ; ; ; ; ; ; ; ; ;

PATTERNS OF PAINT IN CERTAIN
SMALL MISSIONS

,   When next we saw the bright light   /
,   There were several   /
,   /
,   Day had followed itself, for a second half   /
,   /
,   Sun had crawled with experience   /
,   Entwined   /
,   /
,   A motion less fickle than the grievous   /
,   Gold wings   /
,   /
,   It looked as if a piece of breath had been dragged   /
     Through two thoroughly types of dull red dirt

     Till dread   learned a brushstroke

,   History had put it there   to cure it   /
,   /
,   Vibrations from fruit trucks   Earth acting   /
,   /
,   Beyond horror with the joy ideas have   /
,   /
,   A pattern so skinny considering what went on   /
,   /
,   Scooping out half-wings that had been   /
,   Helping a little bit   /
,   /
,   Artist stay general   /

     Mother of god be specific

> > > > > > > > > > >   > > > > > > > > > > > >

San Rafael Arcángel
1817

BREATHING IN CHURCH

A nerveless
Action on the wall of dread:
Hope's fascinating fever.

A door had closed quite quietly (it quietlied);
A busy bell.
Nooned.

It was the spain of you,
The gleaming splosh middle of the day
Of you.   Tent eye.   here.

Were you instructing the pattern?
Did you see the friar
Kneeling in the nosebleed curtain?

Vermilion hills: you see:
Design is about a day,
Paint is about ecstasy

Till despite alive has it
Running in snakes: meaning: waiting
To be astonished—

San Fernando Rey de España
1797

BIRTH OF SYNTAX

Figuring out how to pray with people watching
Whether you close your eyes or not

Not breathing with the small mom sitting not breathing in church
(Baptists don't kneel)

Possible to feel earth's voltage through her white gloves

Mime the stitches where the double ridges collide

Try pressing the main brenda's feel down to do battle with Tucson dirt

Joy comes up through the eyes and causes
Her hair to curl (treble clefs)

The day thing the preacher says over and over not as good
            as a day made by hand

Mourning (from a spelling bee)

Mourning dove outside   _   — — —

(There is a certain amount of mourning you have to do
In Christianity to get up to the level of feeling sad)

Lawn vent smoke from Mr. P's cigarette

A blade of happiness cuts like free verse

A breath makes of each hurt a new religion
It starts interrupting   though in church it was more fun

:: ::

San Carlos Borromeo
1770

NOON CHAIN REPLICA

(A fancy dark goes back and forth
)   Inside a day
(
)   It knows it is smart but at the wrong level
(
)   The meaning noise
(Curly water rattle @@@@
)   Bathing itself in the radiator
(
)   You draw with day toward nylon noon
(Past the garden of profound illness
)   oo
(Doves have it   oo oo oo
)   oo
(Ginkgo hems   Louie Louie we gotta go
)
(o o   forks   spoons (((
)
(We kneel in front of it
)
(They bring their ledgers
)
(Records were burning   Missing breath
)
(You think you lost it
)   It hasn't lost it
(
)   Bring some dirt from middle roses
(
)   Reassemble   ruined stars

San José de Guadalupe
1779

64

7-7-7-7-7-7-7-7-7-7-7-7-7-7-7-7-7-7-7-7-7-7-7-7

A QUOTIDIAN

You worked with next
and then the blur came:
fascinating fever

signaling

someone you loved, in danger—;

was it the trough stone, her crying turned
sideways,

the shield of Granada
that can't cause you pain?

Something keeps missing,
not sure which day—;

hours,   hours,   just ride them—

8*8*8*8*8*8*8*8*8*8*8*8*8*8*8*8*8*8*8*8*8*8*8

San Buenaventura
1782

LEFT EYE

There's a barrier before between

I think they were trying to write their names on it

The rubbed-looking light   a glare of the all along
Had inserted itself into the nerves' lining

Say you saw it   Be alive

As if comprehension were not to blame

As if autonomy were not to blame

And to the you between us   there could be read
            (a   heap of dirt had been pushed up, outside)

In the numberless

Rumorless

Night   the flame narrative   the flame report

+ + +   + + +

San Miguel Arcángel
1797

> > > > x > > > > > > x   the future   x < < < < < < x < < < <

MOTHS WALKING ALONG

+   After a million years you drew a breath

+   Paused till it seemed more accurate
     Not to
+
     A skin between a day and a day is
+   Moths walking along

+   A pointy lurch when it works >>>> to keep
     Wednesday from forever
x
     In the same manner the literal
+
     Fits through any place if you turn it sideways
+   As they fit the cross through slatted doors

+   (A cross is a kiss turned sideways)

+   Others work in the garden
     Spraying surround squash blossoms
+   Whole panamas of water

     Not to be lost in the blend
x   Or consolidate the rose

     That dread or delight

     Some mixture once assured you

     San Juan Bautista
     1797

^^^^^^^^^^^

STORM TRIANGLES

In rough in-
sight

drives bent night
where silk is president

Next day root bound un-
sound the music plant

withered

      That's more
      like it, hills   (comes living

      up to our exile)

      Winter break
      under ache
      we break

      Scratch before the glimpse
      of bird

      erred
      : or : asked
      the trees to stop

whirr: whrrrr:

the descriptions are size, shape, color

needed a pair of quakes
to get us out of here   (a thislessness)

needed three
sides for an ending

      v`v`v`v`v`v`v`v`v`v`v

San Gabriel
1771

+ — +

CHRIST'S HEIGHT

A lily advanced
in three ways,

algebra powder on its tongue;

centuries passed;

a poet
burst with happiness.

Talk to the breathless gardener
about this, take his body
from the uranium castle;

triangle, notify the lily;
I will notify the bee
for you.

Waking design,

suffering confusion,

paling beside
the sided water,
the awkward grid,

we were called
by being
to the savage state. It rings a

polychromatic bee
bell, wing form, count
your threes. The next

time we see him, we'll laugh—

=========== ============

Santa Bárbara
1786

HALF THE HALF-NOCTURNES

I.
—And when the uneven ones had
risen from below interpreting the isinglass

that magnified the last four yellow
apples over the entrance way to

ground (in the lydian mode: *nada*
with the day job, *o canada*

with the night job), their projects
having given way to more baffled

solitudes, a series of vectors pointing
to the cellar stairs, her not

reaching the embassy, your speaking of
barges sailing past the customs houses,

faces in the forcefield that looked
both ways before *a* or *n*

or *y*, long before the triple
world cast itself down in you—

II.
The dream seminars are finishing. Relief
figures emerge from the stone slabs

that leak more abstract petals into
an alphabet. The scribe who sits

and the revenant who is a
soul or sister count the corners

of their little earthly contract. Ibises
shake triangular beaks as they walk,

pecking at pears, ferns, a third
of a revolution. Who recommended fate

to the stars? Her figure shrinks
at the end of the dynasty,

or is it a different figure?
Doesn't matter; western day will take

them outside. A mattress floats by
in a roomier stanza. Everything that

lived still lives, the eaten edge, a

braided night, the missing song
that might have missed the world—

III.
They summoned you when they
removed the kite from the oak,

its tail made of worn leather
and torn hospital sheets. They tried

to contact you in the wool
of the shorn day, when you

stood in the dread of being
held beyond torment, in the absorbed

seed; and now your wounded gardener
works toward summer; don't call him

if you love him; put one
foot in front of the other,

like prose; the violins would play
so, the night ones would say

so; they're loading the notebooks on
a cart that erases its road—

IV.
The latest arrows circle the moon: a
hawk flying around the kissed target

in fog. Blue asterisks appear as
stars on dull railing: the archer

is entering the village of slow
stains, taking the *byt* of *And*

far to the right. The thistles
on his hill are rattling: the self-

reflexive whispers of the archer's assistant
joking with the catenary ashes. Sometimes

outside the black, they knew themselves,
sometimes they started circles where the

history of corners will be written;

unliteral bird, what did you think?
actual moment, where did you go?

V.

VI.
The gleam of the trustees' tower

in the lemon hyphen moonlight. Numbered
cubicles where we stored our doves

and envelopes. (Why did we take
so long to fetch our things—)

How did this existence deepen
and get lighter, disaster dreams confused

with hope like those of friars
carrying a saint's bed higher because

the mission's burning. The last day,

they forget forgetting; the stalled wide
sleep can be what they imagine.

BEFORE MY PENCIL

It took quiet
It took stone

Where the feeling left intensity
It saluted

The mannerism of the curve

Warm saprophyte   Its halo vest

Notched something's antic math

Draw your planet
Enigma
Come back when you have one

Then it crawled among syllables

Then it touched the white fact

ACKNOWLEDGMENTS/NOTES

Grateful acknowledgment is made to the editors of periodicals in which some of these poems have appeared: *American Letters and Commentary, American Poetry Review, Boston Review, Chain, Chicago Review, Citysearch.com, Denver Quarterly, Explosive, Fence, Five Fingers Review, Gulf Coast, Hayden's Ferry Review, Interim, in•tense, The Journal, Mirage # 4 Period(ical), nocturnes (re)view of the literary arts, Pleiades, Ploughshares, Prosodia, Rooms, Sonora Review, syllogism, Tikkun,* and *VOLT.* Some of this work has appeared or will appear in the following anthologies: *American Women Poets in the Twenty-first Century, Best American Poetry 2000, Best American Poetry 2001, Breadloaf Anthology of Contemporary American Poetry, Dorothy Parker's Elbow, Departure of Its Fountains: Five American Women Poets Read From Their Works* (CD), *A Geography of Home, The Literature of California II, Motion,* and *PogTwo.* I am grateful to the Engelhard Foundation for providing a fellowship during the time of this writing.

Many thanks to Bob Hass and Louisa Michaels, to family, dear friends, colleagues and students for their support. Thanks to those who provided suggestions and comments on this work: Joe Ahearn, Cal Bedient, Norma Cole, Patricia Dienstfrey, Forrest Gander, Peter Gizzi, Jorie Graham, Fanny Howe, Marie Howe, Rob Kaufman, Claudia Keelan, Noelle Kocot, Susan Kolodny, Fran Lerner, Steven Madoff, Luke Menand, Laura Mullen, Nan Norene, Geoffrey G. O'Brien, G. E. Patterson, Claudia Rankine, Donald Revell, Lisa Sewell, Chris Sindt, Carol Snow, 'Annah Sobelman, L. B. Thompson, and Dean Young. Thanks to Ed Biglin for tech support, to Cody Gates and Maureen Forys for typesetting and text design, and to Suzanna Tamminen. I am especially grateful to Joshua Clover for assistance in completing this book.

"Hydraulic Mining Survey" is for Gary Snyder. "Sweeping the Interpreter's House" is the title of an engraving by William Blake, who took it from John Bunyan. Quotations from "The Shirley Poem" are from *The Shirley Letters, Being Letters Written in 1851–1852 from the California Mines* by "Dame Shirley" (Louise A. K. S. Clappe). The poem is dedicated to the Reading Group (FB, GC, PD, DLF, DG, DN, ER, CS, CS, GS) and to our Flute Girl. "Songless Era" borrows a phrase from Hildegard of Bingen. "Cascadia" borrows a sentence from Becca Sanchez. "Curved Knowledge" was mixed by Al Greer. "Left Eye" is for Louisa Michaels. "A Quotidian" is for Martha Ronk. The diagrams under "Birth of Lace" are by Lyn Hejinian; the poem is for her and for Natalie Gerber. The other poems from the missions are for Patricia Dienstfrey, Louise Glück, Barbara Guest, and Fanny Howe.

ABOUT THE AUTHOR

Brenda Hillman was born in Tucson, Arizona. After receiving her B.A. at Pomona College, she attended the University of Iowa where she received her M.F.A. She is the author of six collections of poetry and three chapbooks and, with Patricia Dienstfrey, has edited a collection of essays on poetics and motherhood. She lives in the San Francisco Bay Area and serves on the faculty of Saint Mary's College in Moraga.

LIBRARY OF CONGRESS CATALOGING-IN-PUBLICATION DATA

Hillman, Brenda.
    Cascadia / Brenda Hillman.
      p. cm.
    ISBN 0-8195-6491-5 (cloth) -- ISBN 0-8195-6492-3 (pbk.)
    I. Title.
PS3558.I4526 C37 2001
811'.54--dc21   2001035504